THE
LEGACY
OF THE
ANCIENT REALMS

This book is designed to complement the reading experience and bring the reader closer to a work of great impact. This book is not intended to replace the original work, nor does it have the authorization, approval, license or endorsement of the author or publisher of the original work.

Editorial Nova makes no warranties or representations as to the accuracy or completeness of the contents of this book.

All rights reserved, including, without limitation, the right to reproduce this book or any part thereof in any form or by any means, whether electronic, mechanical, or any other means now known or hereafter developed, without the express written permission of the publisher.

THE LEGACY OF THE ANCIENT REALMS.
Copyright © 2025 Editorial Nova.
ISBN: 979-8-3485-1277-4

Contents

Introduction
Part I: The One Ring and its Origin
The Beginning of Everything
The War and the Fall of Sauron
Corruption and the Loss of the Ring
Part II: The Beginning of the Journey
The Shire and Bilbo Baggins
The Wizard Gandalf and the Threat of Sauron
The Council of Elrond
The Fellowship of the Ring
Part III: The Division of the Community and the War
The Journey and the Mines of Moria
Lothlórien and the Betrayal of Boromir
The Riders of Rohan
Frodo and Sam's Journey to Mordor
Part IV: The Final Battle and the Fate of the Ring
The Battle of Helm's Deep
The Attack of the Ents and the Fall of Isengard
The Siege of Minas Tirith
The Road to Mountain Doom
The Destruction of the Ring
Part V: The Return and the End
The Return Home
Epilogue
Final Note
Curiosities
Legal Notice And Copyright
Disclaimer

Introduction

The Lord of the Rings saga is an epic story set in Middle-earth, a world where magic, power, and destiny intertwine. The narrative focuses on the struggle between good and evil, personified in the battle against Sauron , the Dark Lord of Mordor, who seeks to dominate all realms with his corrupting power. The introduction to this book immerses us in a journey where hope and courage are the main weapons against adversity, and where the smallest beings can change the course of history.

The One Ring: At the heart of this story is the One Ring, a relic of power created by Sauron to control the other rings and, by extension, all beings in Middle-earth. This object becomes the central object of the quest and struggle, symbolizing the corruption and temptation of power. Possession of the ring influences those who wear it, leading them down dark paths.

The main characters: The narrative follows a diverse group of characters, each with their own destiny and role in the fight against Sauron . Notable among them are Frodo, a humble hobbit who becomes the bearer of the ring; Gandalf, a wise wizard who guides the fellowship; and Aragorn , the heir to the throne of Gondor , whose destiny is to unify the peoples. Also part of this group are Sam, Merry and Pippin , hobbits who accompany Frodo on his adventure, and Legolas and Gimli, an elf and a dwarf, respectively, who join the cause.

The Fellowship's Journey: The journey of the Fellowship of the Ring is the central axis of the story, an odyssey full of dangers and challenges. From the Shire to the battlefields, the characters face armies of orcs, beasts, and the temptations of power. Along the way, friendship and loyalty are tested, and each character must confront their own inner demons.

The fight for Middle-earth: The war against Sauron is a fight for the freedom and survival of Middle-earth. Kingdoms such as Gondor and Rohan face the forces of Mordor, while elves and dwarves also play an important role in defending the world. The battle is not only a physical confrontation, but also a fight for the ideals and values that represent good.

Core Themes: In addition to adventure, the series explores deeper themes such as the nature of power, corruption, friendship, sacrifice, and hope. Characters must learn to rely on themselves and each other to overcome the challenges they face, and they must make difficult decisions that will have a lasting impact on the world.

An Enduring Legacy: The Lord of the Rings saga is much more than a fantasy story, it is a reflection on the human condition and the struggle between good and evil. Its legacy endures over time as a testament to the power of friendship, courage and hope in times of darkness.

This introduction serves as a starting point to understand the complexity and depth of the story that unfolds throughout the saga, inviting the reader on a journey full of emotion, adventure and reflections on human nature and the power of choice.

Part I:
The One Ring and its Origin

The history of Middle-earth began with the creation of the Great Rings of Power: three for the immortal Elves, seven for the Dwarves, and nine for the Humans. These mystical rings granted power over every race, but what no one knew was that Sauron , the Dark Lord of Mordor, had created one ring to rule them all - a One Ring that would rule over the others. With this power, Sauron became virtually invincible.

However, humans and elves joined forces to confront this dark lord in a crucial battle. In a desperate moment, a young prince named Isildur of the realm of Condor took up a sword and cut off Sauron 's fingers , thus winning the Ring and ending the war. Despite the elven king's insistence that he destroy it, Isildur decided to keep it as a trophy. The Ring, with a will of its own, seduced Isildur and corrupted him, causing his death and then disappearing into a river.

The Ring remained lost until it was found by a hobbit, a race of small, curious beings. This hobbit's cousin, named Smeagol , became obsessed with the treasure and killed it, becoming corrupted by the Ring and becoming Gollum . For thousands of years, Gollum wandered Middle-earth, transforming into an emaciated being obsessed with the Ring. Eventually, the Ring was separated from Gollum and found by another hobbit named Bilbo . Bilbo kept the Ring for many years, unaware of the power it possessed.

The Beginning of Everything

In the early days of Middle-earth, the Rings of Power were forged, artifacts imbued with magic and destined to influence the fate of the various races. Three of these rings were given to the Elves, immortal beings of great wisdom and knowledge. Created to enhance their virtues, these rings were of subtle elegance and power, focused on the preservation and beauty of their world. The Elves, with their deep understanding of nature and magic, used these rings with caution, seeking the harmony and well-being of their realms.

Seven rings were given to the dwarves, master craftsmen and miners, who dwelled deep within the mountains. These rings were imbued with the strength and resilience of rocks and metals, reflecting the dwarves' passion for craftsmanship and the accumulation of wealth. The dwarves, with their ability to transform matter, were drawn to the power of the rings, which allowed them to perfect their creations and expand their dominion over the depths. However, their earthly nature made them susceptible to greed and the desire for possession, sowing the seeds of their downfall.

Nine rings were granted to men, mortals with great ambition and an insatiable desire for power. Closer to human nature, these rings amplified their desires and longings, granting them a strength and influence that was often misused. Men, with their fickle nature and constant quest for dominance, quickly fell under the corrupting influence of the rings, becoming selfish and cruel. These rings became a tool for conquest and oppression, sowing chaos and discord among the realms of men.

But secretly, within the volcano of Mount Doom, Sauron, the Dark Lord of Mordor, forged the One Ring, its purpose being to rule all other Rings and those who would wear them. Crafted from the darkest of magics and Sauron's own will to dominate, this Ring was imbued with his own power, capable of corrupting and subjugating any who wore it. The One Ring became the key to Sauron's power, an instrument of absolute control that would allow him to dominate and enslave all the races of Middle-earth. In creating the Ring, Sauron invested a portion of his soul into it, connecting his fate to the Ring's destiny – a bond that would determine the course of history.

The power of the One Ring lay not only in its ability to control the other rings, but also in its ability to influence the minds and hearts of those who possessed it. The Ring tempted its wearers with promises of greatness and power, corrupting their ambitions and desires until they became possessed. The creation of the One Ring marked a turning point in the history of Middle-earth, ushering in an age of darkness and conflict, and setting in motion a chain of events that would test the bravery and resolve of the different races. Forged from the ambition of a dark lord, this ring became the catalyst for an epic struggle between good and evil, the outcome of which would define the fate of all. The creation of this ring was not only an act of power, but also a harbinger of the darkness to come and a symbol of the corruption that could overtake even the noblest of hearts.

The War and the Fall of Sauron

Following the creation of the Rings of Power and the forging of the One Ring by Sauron , Middle-earth was plunged into an age of darkness and conflict. The Dark Lord's power grew ever greater, threatening to enslave all races under his rule. Faced with this looming threat, Elves and Men, once divided by differences and mistrust, were forced to join forces in an unprecedented alliance. With their combined armies, they faced Sauron 's hordes of Orcs and other evil creatures in a war that would define the future of Middle-earth.

The battle was fierce and merciless, raging across valleys and mountains, with significant losses on both sides. However, the determination and courage of the alliance of Elves and Men managed to drive Sauron 's forces back to the gates of his own fortress in the land of Mordor. In an act of desperation and bravery, the allied armies laid siege to the tower of Barad-dûr , Sauron 's bastion of power . The fighting intensified, with each side fighting to the limits of their strength.

In the heat of battle, when defeat seemed imminent, a young prince named Isildur of the realm of Condor took up a sword and, in an act of daring, cut off the fingers of Sauron , who bore the One Ring. With this act, Sauron 's power faded and his physical body was destroyed. The One Ring, however, remained intact, becoming a symbol of the Dark Lord's downfall and, at the same time, a source of corrupting power that still threatened Middle-earth. The war was over, but the peace would be short-lived.

Although the Elven-king urged him to destroy the Ring in the fires of Mount Doom, the only place where it could be destroyed, Isildur was seduced by its power and kept it as a trophy for himself. The Ring's own will corrupted him, making him believe that he could control it and use it for the good of his realm. Taking the Ring with him, Isildur returned to Gondor , but the consequences of his greed soon caught up with him.

In a moment of carelessness, Isildur was killed and the Ring was lost in the depths of a river. With the loss of the One Ring, Sauron 's shadow seemed to fade, but the threat of his return would always remain. Sauron 's fall was not the end of the struggle, but the beginning of a long and winding road to redemption. Middle-earth now faced an uncertain future, where hope and fear coexisted in a delicate balance.

Isildur 's decision to keep the Ring, rather than destroy it, would mark a turning point in the history of Middle-earth. His mistake would sow the seeds of future conflict and prove that even the greatest heroes can succumb to the temptation of power. The war was over, but the fight for freedom and peace had only just begun. The One Ring, now lost in the depths of Middle-earth, patiently awaited its moment to once again manifest its dark power and influence the fate of all living things. The loss of the Ring was not only a tragedy for Isildur , but also a harbinger of the dangers that still awaited Middle-earth, in a future where Sauron 's shadow might once again fall over the world. The story of the war and Sauron 's downfall reminds us that power, if not wielded with wisdom and virtue, can become a destructive force that corrupts even the noblest of hearts.

Corruption and the Loss of the Ring

Following the fall of Sauron and the loss of the One Ring, Middle-earth entered a period of relative peace, but the shadow of corruption and the power of the Ring still loomed large, waiting patiently for its moment to re-emerge. The fate of Isildur , the prince who cut the Ring from Sauron 's hand , was sealed when, on his way back to Condor, he was killed in an ambush. The One Ring, source of both power and doom, fell from his hands and was lost in a river, adrift beyond the knowledge of Elves, Men, and Dwarves. This event marked the beginning of a new phase in the history of the Ring, where its influence would begin to manifest itself in subtle but deeply corrupting ways.

The Ring lay in the riverbed for a long time, awaiting its destined bearer. It was then that a peculiar being, a hobbit named Smeagol , stumbled upon it while fishing. The hobbit's curious and naive nature led him to pick up the Ring, not understanding its true power or the consequences that its possession would bring. At first, the Ring granted Smeagol certain benefits, such as invisibility and unnatural longevity, but it also transformed him irreversibly. Little by little, the corruption of the Ring took over his body and mind, turning him into a deformed and obsessed creature.

Smeagol was transformed into Gollum , a being consumed by the Ring, no longer viewing it as an object of power, but as his "precious". Gollum 's obsession with the Ring became his raison d'être, leading him to commit heinous acts, such as the murder of his own cousin, who had discovered the jewel before him. Possession of the Ring dragged him into a life of loneliness and suffering, but his dependence on it grew ever deeper and more torturous. Smeagol's former goodness faded, replaced by Gollum's greed and paranoia, who lurked for centuries, hiding from the light and other beings. His transformation was a clear reflection of the Ring's corrupting power, showing how even the most innocent of beings could succumb to its influence.

For centuries, Gollum hid in the depths of Middle-earth, protecting his treasure and waiting for the moment to claim its power. However, fate had other plans. Unexpectedly, the Ring escaped from Gollum's hands, becoming lost once again. This time, the Ring was found by Bilbo Baggins, a hobbit who, during an unexpected journey, stumbled upon Gollum's lair and inadvertently took the jewel. This chance encounter would set in motion a series of events that would change the fate of Middle-earth forever, as the Ring, after a long wait, would once again manifest its corrupting power, this time through the figure of a peaceful hobbit who loved the good life.

Bilbo's encounter with the Ring represented a turning point in the jewel's history, for although the hobbit did not immediately succumb to its power, its possession marked the beginning of a new phase in the struggle for control of the Ring. From this moment on, Middle-earth would be embroiled in a series of conflicts involving all races, as the Ring's power would attract the attention of dark forces that wished to seize it. The Ring, after centuries of darkness and silence, was once again on the scene, ready to awaken ancient ambitions and unleash a new era of wars and conflicts. Bilbo's loss and subsequent finding of the Ring marked the beginning of a new adventure, where the fate of the world would be left in the hands of small beings, but with a determination that would defy darkness itself.

Part II:
The Beginning of the Journey

Sixty years after Bilbo found the Ring, the story moves to the Shire, a peaceful place where hobbits live. It is here that we meet Frodo, a hobbit who is visited by Gandalf the Grey, a pleasant-looking wizard. The occasion of this visit is the celebration of Bilbo 's birthday , who decides to throw a big party and invite everyone. During the celebration, other important characters appear, such as Sam, a shy-looking hobbit, and the mischievous Pippin and Merry.

The party goes on as normal, with dancing, ale and fireworks. At the end of the night, Bilbo offers some emotional farewell words and, to everyone's surprise, puts on the ring and turns invisible. Bilbo decides to leave the Shire forever, but is intercepted by Gandalf, who asks him to leave the ring, as it is now the responsibility of his nephew Frodo. Bilbo finds it hard to leave him, but eventually agrees. Gandalf reveals to Frodo that he must now keep the ring.

However, the tranquility of the Shire is threatened by the return of Sauron , who is raising an army of orcs in search of the ring. Gollum , who had been captured and tortured by Sauron 's forces , reveals the location of Bilbo and the Shire. Faced with this threat, Gandalf asks Frodo to undertake a journey to a village called April , where they will meet. Frodo is helped by his friend Sam, who accompanies him on his journey by being a gossip. Meanwhile, Gandalf heads to Aysén Garth , where Saruman , another wizard, lives.

In Aysén Garth , Gandalf discovers that Saruman has been corrupted by Sauron and is helping him raise an army of orcs. Rumours spread that an even more powerful enemy is at work. Saruman attacks Gandalf, but he escapes. Meanwhile, Frodo and Sam begin their journey and meet Merry and Pippin , who join them on their adventure. Danger sets in when Sauron 's warriors, Nazgûl , appear on demonic horses. The hobbits escape the Nazgûl and head to an inn where they are supposed to meet Gandalf.

At the inn, Pippin accidentally reveals Frodo's identity, alerting the Nazgûl . To avoid discovery, Frodo puts on the Ring and becomes invisible, seeing the Eye of Sauron for the first time . The Nazgûl attack the inn, but a mysterious, bearded man appears to protect the hobbits. This man leads them to a safe inn, and then decides to take them to the elves' lair at Rivendell , where they will surely know what to do with the Ring. Along the way, the hobbits are attacked by the Nazgûl , and their leader wounds Frodo with a poisoned razor.

An elf named Arwen rescues Frodo and takes him to Rivendell , where he is healed. Once recovered, Frodo meets with Gandalf, who explains that he was able to escape Saruman thanks to the help of some animals that helped him summon eagles. In Rivendell , the leaders of the different races meet, including the elf king Elrond , who agrees that the ring must be destroyed. At this meeting it is decided that the ring must be taken to Mountain Doom, the only place where it can be destroyed.

Among the leaders who offer to accompany Frodo on his quest are Aragorn , a mysterious man who is a descendant of Isildur , Legolas , an elf archer, and Gimli, a dwarf. Also joining the quest is Boromir , son of the steward of Gondor . Frodo binds his eggs and decides that he will be responsible for carrying the ring to Mount Doom. Thus the Fellowship of the Ring is formally formed, and sets out from Rivendell on a mission to save Middle-earth. Before departing, Bilbo gives Frodo his sword, which turns blue when orcs are near, and a mithril mail vest . Bilbo is nearly corrupted by the ring again upon seeing it. Thus begins the perilous journey of the Fellowship of the Ring.

The Shire and Bilbo Baggins

A peaceful and quiet place inhabited by hobbits, the Shire is characterized by a slow pace of life, where worries are few and simple pleasures are highly valued. Life in the Shire is filled with feasting, visiting friends, and tending to their well-tended gardens and fields. Known for their love of good food, drink, and celebration, hobbits enjoy a quiet existence, oblivious to the dangers that lurk in the outside world. Their society is peaceful and traditional, with a deep sense of community and respect for ancient ways.

In this serene setting, Bilbo Baggins, a somewhat eccentric but highly respected hobbit, decides to celebrate his birthday with a big party. Inviting all his friends and neighbours, Bilbo prepares an event that becomes the centre of attention for the whole Shire. The party is a reflection of the joy and simplicity of hobbit life, with plenty of food, ale, music and fireworks. The guests enjoy the celebration, sharing laughter, dancing and anecdotes. Among the attendees, there are some characters who, unwittingly, are destined to play an important role in the future of Middle-earth, such as his nephew Frodo, and his young friends Sam, Pippin and Merry.

At the end of the evening, Bilbo addresses his guests to give a farewell speech. With emotional words, he lets it be known that he is about to embark on a journey, a new chapter in his life that will take him far from the Shire. To everyone's surprise, as he speaks, Bilbo puts on a ring he was carrying with him and becomes invisible.

This act causes surprise and confusion among those present, who do not understand what has just happened. The ability to become invisible is a reflection of the power of the One Ring, which Bilbo had found years ago, but which until now he had not used in public.

After turning invisible, Bilbo takes advantage of the confusion to sneak away from the party unnoticed and return home to pack his belongings and leave the Shire for good. However, his departure is interrupted by the arrival of Gandalf, the wizard who had come to the party. Gandalf, aware of the danger posed by the One Ring, asks Bilbo to leave it behind, as it is now too great a burden for him. Bilbo , although he finds it difficult to part with the ring, agrees and gives it to Gandalf, who in turn entrusts it to Frodo, Bilbo 's nephew . With this delivery, the Ring passes into the hands of a new bearer and a series of events is set in motion that will shake Middle-earth.

Gandalf explains to Frodo that he is now responsible for guarding the Ring, without fully revealing the true nature of the Ring or the danger that its possession entails. The wizard warns him of the return of Sauron , who is searching for the Ring with the help of his army of Orcs. Aware of the danger, Gandalf asks Frodo to undertake a journey to a village called April , where they will meet to discuss the future of the Ring and the best way to protect it. With this decision, Frodo's quiet life is turned upside down and the hobbit, unwittingly , becomes the central axis of an adventure that will define the destiny of Middle-earth.

Thus, the peaceful life of the Shire is interrupted by the arrival of events that will test the courage and determination of the hobbits. Bilbo 's birthday party , which had begun as a joyful celebration, becomes the starting point of a journey full of dangers and challenges. Bilbo 's decision to leave the Shire and give the Ring to

Frodo marks the beginning of a new era in the history of Middle-earth, an era where the fate of the world will be in the hands of a small hobbit who must face the growing darkness that looms over him and everything he knows.

The Wizard Gandalf and the Threat of Sauron

Gandalf, the grey-bearded wizard with a piercing gaze, becomes the bearer of news that will change the fate of Middle-earth and the life of the young hobbit Frodo. After Bilbo 's departure and the delivery of the Ring, Gandalf decides to reveal the truth about this mysterious object, explaining its origin and the magnitude of the power it contains. The revelation comes as a cold shower for Frodo, who until then was unaware of the true nature of the relic and the dangers that accompany it. Gandalf explains to Frodo that the ring is actually the One Ring, created by the Dark Lord Sauron to control all the other rings of power. He explains that this ring has a will of its own, seeking to return to its creator.

The tranquility of the Shire is threatened by the imminent return of Sauron , whose power grows with each passing day. Sauron , the dark lord of Mordor, mobilizes his armies of orcs and begins a relentless quest to recover the One Ring, which will restore him to his former power and allow him to dominate all Middle-earth. Sauron 's ambition is as great as his cruelty, and his followers, the orcs, are fearsome and ruthless beings who will stop at nothing to do their master's bidding. Middle-earth shudders before the shadow of evil that spreads from Mordor, and the hope of the free peoples begins to fade.

Sauron 's quest for the One Ring is not a random process, but is based on information gained through the torture of Gollum , the creature who for years had been corrupted by the Ring. Gollum , who had once possessed the Ring, reveals the location of Bilbo and the Shire, information that endangers the safety and peace of the hobbits. Gollum's confession unleashes the fury of Sauron, who orders his minions to head to the Shire to recover the Ring, no matter the means necessary. This information reaches the ears of Gandalf, who understands that the situation is critical and that it is necessary to act quickly to protect Frodo and the Ring.

Faced with the imminent threat, Gandalf decides that Frodo must undertake a journey to the village of April, where they will meet to devise a plan and find a way to protect the One Ring. Frodo's decision to leave the Shire marks the beginning of an adventure that will take him to unknown places and face unimaginable dangers. Frodo's journey, accompanied by his faithful friend Sam, becomes a race against time, with Sauron's army hot on his heels. With each step they take, the hobbits delve deeper into an increasingly dark and dangerous world, where hope is a scarce commodity. Frodo's courage is put to the test, because the young hobbit is not accustomed to the hardships of a journey.

As Frodo ventures out on his journey, Gandalf heads to Isengard, the fortress of the wizard Saruman, intending to seek his advice and support in the fight against Sauron. Gandalf, in his wisdom, is confident that Saruman, a powerful and respected wizard, will share his concern and join the cause of the free peoples. Upon arriving at Isengard, however, Gandalf discovers to his horror that Saruman has been corrupted by Sauron's power and has become his ally. Saruman's betrayal is a devastating blow to Gandalf and to the hope of Middle-earth, for the forces of evil now have the support of one of the most powerful wizards. Saruman attacks Gandalf, proving that he is on Sauron's side.

Gandalf's decision to go to Isengard marks a turning point in the story. The revelation of Saruman's betrayal forces the free peoples to face the reality that the war against Sauron will be even more difficult than they thought. With each step, Sauron's threat becomes more palpable, while the hope of Middle-earth slowly fades. The path that awaits Frodo and the fellowship that will join his cause will be fraught with danger, but their bravery and determination will be the last hope against the darkness that looms over Middle-earth. Frodo's journey and Saruman's betrayal are two events that intertwine to form a future full of challenges.

The Council of Elrond

The quest for the One Ring intensifies when Gandalf discovers the betrayal of Saruman , his former ally and fellow wizard. This discovery marks a turning point in the fight against evil, as the alliance between Saruman and Sauron greatly increases the power of darkness and threatens the stability of Middle-earth. Saruman 's betrayal is a devastating blow to the hope of the free peoples, who must now face a doubly dangerous threat. Meanwhile, the hobbits - Frodo, Sam, Merry, and Pippin - continue their journey, oblivious to the full extent of evil's power and the corruption that has spread even among those who considered themselves allies.

The pursuit of the Nazgûl , Sauron 's most fearsome winged wraiths and servants , becomes a constant nightmare for the hobbits. These dark warriors, mounted on winged beasts, tirelessly track the bearers of the One Ring, drawing ever closer to their goal. The hobbits, aware of the danger that lurks, are forced to constantly flee and hide, seeking refuge in inns and safe places. Fear and uncertainty grip them, but their determination to fulfill their mission gives them the strength to continue on. The pursuit of the Nazgûl intensifies when the hobbits arrive at an inn, where Pippin reveals information about Frodo, which alerts their pursuers.

Amidst the confusion and danger, Frodo is forced to use the One Ring to escape the Nazgûl , but in doing so he sees a vision of the Eye of Sauron , an image of fire and destruction that reveals to him the full extent of his enemy's power. Wearing the ring exposes Frodo to the Dark Lord's power and allows the Dark Lord to see him, further exacerbating the situation. The experience is terrifying for Frodo, who realises that the Ring is not only an object of power, but also a trap that could lead to his own destruction. The vision of the Eye of Sauron marks a pivotal moment in Frodo's adventure, for he realises that his task will be more difficult than he imagined.

At a critical moment, when the Nazgûl are about to reach the hobbits, a mysterious man, a hairy and bearded fellow, appears to rescue and protect them. This man, whose identity is kept secret for the moment, shows great skill and bravery in fighting the dark wraiths, guiding the hobbits to a safer place. The bearded man hides them in another inn and then decides to take them to Rivendell, the refuge of the elves, for he understands that they will have the knowledge and wisdom to help them in their mission. The appearance of this mysterious man is a ray of hope in the darkness that surrounds the hobbits, but their path remains uncertain and full of dangers.

On the road to Rivendell, Frodo is severely wounded by the leader of the Nazgûl, whose weapon contains a deadly poison. The wound puts Frodo's life in danger, and his companions must rush to bring him to the elves, who have the ability to heal him. Time becomes a crucial factor, and each passing minute puts the hobbit's life at greater risk. However, at the most critical moment, an elf named Arwen appears and takes Frodo away on her horse, carrying him to Rivendell at full speed. Along the way, she proves herself a brave warrior by fighting off the Nazgûl in a river, protecting Frodo from their clutches.

Eventually, Frodo reaches Rivendell, where he is healed by the Elven-king Elrond. A place of beauty and wisdom, the Elven-king offers the hobbits respite from the pursuit of the Nazgûl. Frodo recovers from his wounds and prepares to face the challenges that lie ahead. In Rivendell, Frodo reunites with Gandalf, who has escaped from Saruman , and with other leaders and champions of the free races. The meeting at Rivendell marks the beginning of a new phase in the fight against the darkness, for it will decide the fate of the One Ring and all of Middle-earth.

The arrival of the leaders and champions of the allied races in Rivendell is a pivotal moment in the fight against Sauron . Notable characters include: Boromir , the son of the steward of Gondor , a brave but impulsive man; Legolas , the elven prince of Mirkwood, a skilled and loyal archer; and Gimli, a strong and determined dwarf. The presence of these leaders marks a moment of unity between the different races, who are all threatened by the same darkness. At this council, the fate of the One Ring is discussed, and it is decided that the only way to defeat Sauron is to destroy the ring at Mountain Doom, the place where it was forged.

The decision to take the Ring to Mount Doom is a momentous one, as it involves a dangerous journey fraught with uncertainty. Frodo volunteers to carry the Ring, accepting the weight of responsibility that this quest entails. From that moment on, the fate of Middle-earth rests on the shoulders of a young hobbit, who must face unimaginable dangers to destroy the One Ring and defeat Sauron . At this moment, the identity of the bearded man is also revealed: Aragorn , heir to the throne of Gondor and descendant of Isildur . It is revealed that Aragorn had exiled himself out of fear of the Ring's power, but is now ready to reclaim his inheritance and fight for the good of Middle-earth.

The Council of Elrond marks the beginning of the formation of the Fellowship of the Ring, a group of heroes of different races united by a common goal: to destroy the One Ring and defeat Sauron . With the help of Gandalf, Aragorn , Legolas , Gimli, Boromir , and the hobbits Frodo, Sam, Merry, and Pippin , the journey to Mountain Doom begins, a path full of dangers and challenges, but one that offers the only hope for the salvation of Middle-earth. At this moment, Bilbo gives Frodo his sword, which lights up in the presence of orcs, and his mithril mail vest . The chapter ends with the departure of the Fellowship, marking the beginning of an adventure that will test the bravery and determination of all its members.

The Fellowship of the Ring

The fate of the One Ring becomes the focus of intense debate in Rivendell. The leaders and champions of the free races, gathered in council, argue heatedly over possible solutions to confront the threat of Sauron. The power of the Ring is undeniable, and the temptation to use it for one's own good or for the greater good causes disagreement and tension among those present. The dwarf Gimli attempts to destroy it with his axe, but the Ring remains undamaged, proving that it can only be destroyed in the place where it was created. Some propose using the Ring to fight Sauron, believing that its power might be the only way to defeat him. However, others, wiser and aware of the corruption the Ring exerts, strongly oppose this idea, knowing that succumbing to its power would only lead to doom. The discussion rages on, but in the end, the conclusion is reached that the Ring cannot be controlled, and its existence represents a constant danger to Middle-earth.

In the midst of the debate, Frodo makes a momentous decision by volunteering to take the One Ring to Mount Doom, the only place where it can be destroyed. The hobbit, aware of the danger involved in this mission, understands that the fate of Middle-earth depends on him. His courage and determination surprise everyone present, as Frodo is neither a warrior nor a leader, but a simple hobbit. However, his humility and noble spirit make him the only one capable of assuming this great responsibility. With his offer, Frodo becomes the bearer of the ring, a title that will mark his life and lead him to face the greatest dangers. Frodo's decision is received with admiration and respect by all the members of the council, who understand that he has assumed a weight that few would be able to bear.

Following Frodo's decision, the Fellowship of the Ring is formed, a group of heroes of different races who agree to accompany the hobbit on his dangerous mission. The fellowship is made up of Gandalf, the wise wizard and guide; Aragorn, the heir to the throne of Gondor, a brave and just leader; Legolas, the elf prince, a skilled and loyal archer; Gimli, the dwarf, a strong and determined warrior; Boromir, the son of the steward of Gondor, a brave but impulsive man; and the hobbits Sam, Merry and Pippin, Frodo's loyal friends. The union of these characters marks a crucial moment in the fight against evil, as it represents the unity of the free races in Middle-earth. The members of the fellowship, although different in their origins and personalities, share the same goal: to destroy the One Ring and defeat Sauron. Although at first they do not get along, the common mission makes them become friends.

Before setting out, Bilbo, the old hobbit who found the ring in the past, has an emotional meeting with his nephew Frodo. At this meeting, Bilbo gives Frodo his sword, which turns blue when there are orcs around, and his mithril mail vest, a light but strong armor that will protect him on his journey. These gifts are not only material objects, but also symbols of Bilbo's legacy and the connection between generations of hobbits. The sword, which in the past was used by Bilbo in his own adventures, will now serve Frodo in his fight against evil. Likewise, the mail shirt, made of mithril, will protect him from the dangers that lurk on his path. The moment when Bilbo gives these objects to Frodo symbolizes the passing of the torch between generations and the continuity in the fight against darkness. Also, upon seeing the ring, Bilbo is almost carried away by its power, but controls himself and walks away from it.

The Fellowship of the Ring, burdened with hope and courage, prepares to embark on its journey to Mount Doom. The path that awaits them is uncertain and fraught with danger, but the members of the fellowship are united by a common purpose: to destroy the One Ring and defeat Sauron . The journey of the fellowship represents the beginning of a new phase in the fight against darkness, where the courage and determination of each will be put to the test. The formation of the fellowship and the delivery of Bilbo 's gifts to Frodo mark the end of this chapter, but also the beginning of a great adventure, where the fate of Middle-earth will be defined. The chapter ends with the heroes setting out towards their destination, leaving behind the safety of Rivendell and entering into the dangers that await them.

Part III:
The Division of the Community and the War

The Fellowship of the Ring, having overcome numerous hardships, faces a crisis that tests its unity and resolve. The dangers of the journey, the dark forces that pursue them, and the growing power of the One Ring begin to undermine trust and loyalty among its members. Boromir , consumed by ambition and the desire to use the ring to defend his realm, succumbs to temptation and attempts to take it from Frodo. This act of betrayal marks a turning point in the story, where the fellowship is divided and each member must go their own way. Distrust and fear grip the group, forcing Frodo to make a difficult decision that will change the course of events.

Frodo, aware of the danger that the Ring represents for his companions and for himself, decides to continue his journey alone towards Mordor, accompanied only by Sam, his faithful friend and companion. Frodo's decision is based on the conviction that he is the only one capable of resisting the temptation of the Ring and carrying out his mission to destroy it. In this way, Frodo and Sam separate from the rest of the fellowship, beginning their own journey towards Mount Doom. The separation of the fellowship marks the beginning of a new stage in the story, where each member will face their own challenges and tests. Aragorn , Legolas and Gimli undertake the search for the hobbits Merry and Pippin , who are captured by the orcs, while Frodo and Sam delve into the heart of darkness.

Meanwhile, war rages across Middle-earth. Sauron's forces, led by Saruman, advance upon the realms of Men, wreaking destruction and death. Saruman, corrupted by power, has betrayed his former allies and raised an army of Orcs to subdue all the free peoples. Gandalf, resurrected as Gandalf the White, emerges as the leader of the resistance against the forces of darkness. Gandalf, with his wisdom and power, leads the free peoples in battle against Sauron, uniting Men, Elves, and Dwarves in a common front against evil. Middle-earth becomes a battlefield where each race must fight for its survival.

War rages across Middle-earth, with epic battles and heroic acts of bravery. Aragorn, revealed to be the heir to the throne of Gondor, leads men in the defense of their kingdoms, fighting with courage and honor. The Elves, led by Legolas, also join the battle, demonstrating their prowess in combat. The Dwarves, led by Gimli, fight with their characteristic strength and determination. The Ents, the living trees of Middle-earth, join the battle, razing Saruman's fortress at Isengard. The war is relentless, but hope is kept alive by the resistance of the free peoples. At Helm's Deep, the King of Rohan and his people take refuge and fight off the Orcs, until they are rescued by Gandalf and the army of Rohan, including Éowyn, the king's niece.

Frodo and Sam, on their journey to Mordor, are forced to rely on Gollum, the creature corrupted by the Ring, who guides them through dangerous paths. Torn between his desire for the Ring and his fidelity to Frodo, Gollum becomes a complex and ambiguous figure. Gollum's presence creates tension between Frodo and Sam, as the former begins to feel pity for the creature, while the latter distrusts his intentions. The relationship between Frodo, Sam, and Gollum becomes a reflection of the internal struggle each character wages against corruption and darkness. While Frodo is weakened by the power of the Ring, Sam remains his faithful companion, who watches over him and encourages him to continue on his quest.

Amidst war and division, hope persists in the figure of Aragorn , who reveals himself as the leader who will unite the free peoples and guide Middle-earth to victory. Despite his self-exile and doubts, Aragorn decides to accept his destiny as king and set out on the path to reclaim his throne. Aragorn , as a descendant of Isildur , becomes the only hope to defeat Sauron and restore order to Middle-earth. Middle-earth prepares for a final battle that will decide its fate.

The Journey and the Mines of Moria

The Fellowship of the Ring sets out on their perilous journey, facing numerous obstacles and challenges from the start. Dangers lurk at every turn, and Orcs, Sauron's servants, are soon on the scene, pursuing the heroes on their way to Mount Doom. Sauron's spies watch the group's every move, and attacks become more frequent. The fellowship must overcome not only the difficult terrain, but also the constant threat of the Orcs, who seek at all costs to seize the One Ring. In their attempt to escape these dangers, the members of the fellowship must make difficult decisions that lead them to dark and mysterious places.

Faced with increasing persecution by the Orcs, the Fellowship of the Ring decides to take an alternate route and enters the mines of Moria, an ancient Dwarven kingdom abandoned centuries ago. The entrance to the mines is hidden and guarded, but with the help of Gandalf, the heroes manage to find their way. However, the mines of Moria are not a safe place, for in their depths dwell ancient creatures and unimaginable dangers. As they enter the dark passages, the members of the fellowship feel the oppression and mystery of the place, a ruined kingdom that holds ancient secrets and latent dangers. The mines, once a place of splendor and grandeur, have now become a labyrinth of tunnels and passages where darkness reigns.

Deep within the mines of Moria, the Fellowship of the Ring is attacked by a horde of Orcs, who have discovered their presence in the underground realm. The battle is intense and bloody, and the members of the Fellowship must fight with all their might to survive. Legolas demonstrates his skill with the bow, cutting down numerous enemies with his well-aimed arrows. Gimli, with his axe, faces the Orcs with bravery and strength. Aragorn, with his sword, leads the Fellowship into battle, defending his companions and fighting with honor. However, the Orcs' force is numerous, and the heroes must draw on all their skill and determination to survive the attack. Amidst the chaos of the battle, the noise awakens an ancient creature that dwells deep within the mines.

Amid the heat of battle, a terrifying figure emerges from the depths: a Balrog, a demon of fire and shadow, and attacks the Fellowship of the Ring. The Balrog is a creature of great power, capable of destroying all in its path, and its presence in the mines of Moria poses a mortal danger to the heroes. Gandalf confronts the Balrog, attempting to stop its advance and protect his companions, and the two engage in an epic battle of power. The fight between Gandalf and the Balrog takes place on the bridge of Khazad-dûm, a narrow and dangerous place where the earth trembles and flames consume all. At the climax of the battle, Gandalf confronts the Balrog in a duel of power.

In an act of supreme bravery, Gandalf confronts the Balrog on the bridge of Khazad-dûm, preventing the beast from advancing and reaching his companions. In a dramatic moment, Gandalf manages to break the bridge, sending the Balrog plummeting into the abyss, but the creature, in its fall, drags the wizard with it. Gandalf's fall into the abyss marks a tragic moment for the Fellowship of the Ring, who watch in despair as their guide and mentor disappears into the darkness. The loss of Gandalf generates a feeling of hopelessness in the fellowship, who feel lost and helpless in the face of their guide's death. However, Gandalf's bravery serves as an inspiration to the heroes, who continue their journey towards Mountain Doom, despite adversity.

The fall of Gandalf marks a turning point in the story, where the members of the Fellowship of the Ring must move forward without their guidance and mentor. Gandalf's death forces them to take on greater responsibility and rely on their own strength. The fellowship, devastated by the loss of their friend and leader, must continue their mission, carrying with them the memory of his sacrifice. Despite the pain and uncertainty, the Fellowship of the Ring continues on its perilous journey, guided by the spirit of bravery and hope that Gandalf passed on to them. The road that awaits them is full of challenges, but the heroes know that the fate of Middle-earth depends on their courage and determination. The battle in the mines and the loss of Gandalf mark the end of this chapter, but also the beginning of a new stage in the fight against darkness, where the fellowship faces uncertainty and adversity.

Lothlórien and the Betrayal of Boromir

Following the tragic loss of Gandalf in the mines of Moria, the Fellowship of the Ring, plunged into sadness and uncertainty, continues its journey south. They reach the magical forest of Lothlórien, a haven of peace and beauty ruled by the elf Galadriel . This forest, protected by her power, becomes a haven of tranquility for the weary travelers, who are received with hospitality and courtesy. The atmosphere of Lothlórien is serene and ethereal, a stark contrast to the dangers and darkness they have faced on their journey. The fellowship finds temporary respite, surrounded by the natural beauty and ancient magic of the elven forest, a place that seems alien to the evils that plague the rest of Middle-earth.

In Lothlórien, the fellowship is privileged to meet the powerful and wise Galadriel , who possesses a clear vision of the future and the dangers that lie ahead. Galadriel greets the travelers with kindness and wisdom, offering them counsel and guidance on their quest. She understands the magnitude of the One Ring's power and the danger it poses to all, warning each member of the fellowship of the temptation it can exert on their hearts. Galadriel , with her piercing vision, reveals each one's deepest fears and desires, showing them the true nature of the struggle they face. Her words serve as a reminder of the importance of humility and resilience in the face of darkness. The fellowship, after this encounter, is faced with their own fragility and the trials they will have to overcome on their way.

Despite Galadriel 's warnings , the temptation of the One Ring begins to exert its power over some members of the fellowship. Boromir , the warrior of Gondor , becomes increasingly consumed by the desire to use the ring to defend his realm. His ambition and fear of defeat lead him to succumb to the temptation, seeing in the ring a tool to gain power. Boromir's internal struggle sharpens as the ring corrupts him, leading him to doubt his companions and plot to seize the object. His obsession becomes a latent danger to the fellowship, generating tension and mistrust among its members. The others watch with concern as Boromir's goodness fades, giving way to the darkness of the ring.

Frodo, aware of the growing danger that the ring represents for his companions, makes the difficult decision to continue his journey alone towards Mordor, accompanied only by Sam, his faithful friend. This decision is based on the conviction that he is the only one capable of resisting the temptation of the ring and fulfilling his mission to destroy it. Frodo's determination is reinforced by seeing Boromir's growing greed and the vulnerability of his friends before the power of the ring. The separation of the fellowship marks a new turning point in the story, where each character must face his own destiny. Frodo and Sam, separated from the group, embark on a solitary journey, guided by hope and the determination to fulfill their mission.

In a last attempt to seize the ring, Boromir attacks Frodo, revealing his treachery and his excessive ambition. However, this act is thwarted by Frodo's bravery, who escapes with the help of Sam, managing to prevent the warrior from taking the ring. After his failed attack, Boromir understands the gravity of his actions and the magnitude of his mistake. In a final act of redemption, Boromir defends Merry and Pippin from an attack by orcs, sacrificing his life to save the hobbits. His death represents a tragic end for a warrior who succumbed to temptation, but also a sign of his repentance and bravery. The loss of Boromir shocks the community and leads them to reflect on the consequences of power and greed.

Boromir's death and Frodo's separation, Sam, true to his promise, follows his master, proving his loyalty and unconditional friendship. Sam does not abandon Frodo on his path, despite the dangers and difficulties they must face. Sam's determination to support Frodo until the end becomes an example of friendship and sacrifice. Sam, despite not having the power or skill of other characters, is the supporting force that drives Frodo to continue his mission. Frodo and Sam's journey, despite the loneliness, will be full of hope and courage, guided by the light of their unbreakable friendship. The story continues, while the fate of Middle-earth hangs in the balance, and the forces of darkness seek to impose their power over the entire free world.

The Riders of Rohan

Following the separation of the Fellowship of the Ring, Aragorn , Legolas and Gimli, driven by their loyalty and friendship, begin a relentless pursuit of the orcs who have captured Merry and Pippin . The determination of these three warriors drives them to great distances, following the trail of their hobbit friends through dangerous and wild terrain. The journey is arduous and exhausting, but their hope of rescuing their companions drives them onward. The urgency of the mission becomes increasingly apparent, as they know that the fate of the hobbits lies in the hands of the orcs, servants of evil. Aragorn , Legolas and Gimli's search becomes a race against time, as they confront the difficulties of the terrain and the threat of encounters with dark forces.

Meanwhile, the Orcs, led by Saruman 's forces , are taking Merry and Pippin towards Isengard , the wizard's stronghold. Saruman intends to use the hobbits as pawns in his plan to take over Middle-earth. The capture of Merry and Pippin represents a victory for the forces of darkness, and their fate becomes uncertain as they approach the evil wizard's lair. The hobbits, despite their size and apparent frailty, remain brave and hopeful, seeking any opportunity to escape their captors. The road to Isengard becomes a test of their endurance and loyalty to one another, as they confront the cruelty and darkness of their captors.

In Rohan, the realm of the Riders, King Théoden finds himself under the control of Saruman , who has weakened him with his manipulations and spells. Saruman 's influence is manifested through Gríma Wormtongue, the king's advisor, who poisons Théoden's mind and isolates him from his people and from reality.

The kingdom of Rohan sinks into chaos and hopelessness, while the king becomes increasingly apathetic and vulnerable to Saruman's evil. Saruman's manipulation of King Théoden exemplifies the power of darkness to corrupt even the most powerful, plunging an entire kingdom into the shadow of despair. The once strong kingdom falls into decline and its people begin to lose hope, while the Orcs advance with their sinister plans.

At a critical moment, Gandalf, who has returned as the White Wizard, arrives in Rohan to free King Théoden from Saruman's grasp. The wizard uses his power and wisdom to dispel the spells holding the king captive and restore his mind and spirit. Gandalf's arrival marks a turning point in the history of Rohan, as the king regains his strength and leadership. Théoden's release is a moment of hope for the realm, which begins to mobilize to confront the threat of Saruman. The truth is revealed, and hope returns to the realm, as the people prepare for the coming struggle.

Following his release, King Théoden, motivated by the urgency of the situation and the advice of Gandalf, decides to lead his people to Helm's Deep, a fortress that he hopes will provide them with refuge from the advancing Orcs. The king's decision is based on the need to defend his people and prepare for the coming battle. The army of Rohan moves towards Helm's Deep, hoping to resist Saruman's attack. Aragorn decides to stay with the king and his people while Gandalf sets out in search of reinforcements. The march to Helm's Deep becomes a test of the bravery and determination of the people of Rohan, as they prepare to face the darkness that looms over Middle-earth. The bravery of the people and the leadership of the king become a beacon of hope in times of despair.

During the journey to Helm's Deep, an emotional connection is revealed between Aragorn and the king's niece, Éowyn . The bond between the two is born of admiration and mutual respect, as they prepare for the coming battle. Aragorn finds himself torn between his love for the immortal elf Arwen and his emerging connection to Éowyn . Battle looms, but so do new hopes and feelings that add a new dimension to the story. As the kingdom of Rohan prepares for war, the fate of Middle-earth still hangs in the balance, with darkness threatening to plunge everything into shadow and despair.

Frodo and Sam's Journey to Mordor

After being separated from the Fellowship of the Ring, Frodo and Sam find themselves alone, facing the dangers and challenges of their journey to Mordor. Along the way, they encounter a strange and wretched creature named Gollum , a being corrupted by the power of the Ring, who has been following Frodo since his departure from the Shire. Gollum is a complex figure, marked by suffering and obsession, who arouses both compassion and distrust in Frodo. Despite Sam's initial opposition, Frodo decides to give him a chance, sensing that Gollum can guide him through the dangerous paths that lead to Mordor. Gollum 's presence adds a new dynamic to the story, becoming a character who oscillates between help and betrayal, reflecting Frodo's own internal struggle against the corrupting power of the Ring.

Gollum , with his knowledge of hidden paths, leads Frodo and Sam through the Dead Marshes, a dark and dangerous place, full of traps and evil presences. This journey tests the hobbits' endurance and mettle, who must confront the difficult terrain and the constant threat of dangers that lurk in the darkness. Despite the difficulties, Frodo and Sam persevere on their way, driven by their determination to fulfill their mission and destroy the ring. During their journey, Gollum shows a mixture of usefulness and menace, being both a guide and a danger to the hobbits, his presence generates a constant tension that affects the relationship between Frodo and Sam.

Amid the darkness and danger that surrounds their journey, a new and fearsome enemy emerges: the Witch-king of Angmar, leader of the Nazgûl, who pursue Frodo in order to seize the ring. The presence of this enemy, mounted on a winged beast, increases the pressure and anguish on the hobbits' path, who must avoid his capture at all costs. The Witch-king represents a direct and powerful threat, which highlights the magnitude of the dangers that Frodo and Sam must face in their mission to destroy the ring.

Gollum's complexity is manifested through his two personalities: Sméagol, his former self, who tries to show kindness, and Gollum, the Ring-corrupted personality who seeks to recover his "precious" at all costs. This duality creates confusion in Frodo, who seeks to trust Sméagol, but must remain vigilant against Gollum's malice. This internal struggle of Gollum reflects the struggle between light and darkness, a central theme in the story, which becomes more intense as the hobbits advance on their path towards Mordor.

In an unexpected turn of events, Frodo, Sam, and Gollum are captured by Faramir, brother of the deceased Boromir, and his men. Faramir, despite being a man of Gondor, displays a sense of honor and justice, as well as a strong resistance to the temptation of the Ring, so he decides not to use it as a weapon. The capture tests the loyalty and bravery of the hobbits, who must convince Faramir that their mission is to destroy the Ring and that they will not use it to gain power. Faramir, after hearing Frodo's story and observing his determination, feels empathy for their struggle and decides to help them on their way to destroying the Ring.

Following their capture and subsequent encounter with Faramir, and realizing the nobility of Frodo's purpose, Frodo decides to let them go, confident that the path they have chosen is the right one. This decision marks a pivotal moment in the story, where kindness and compassion triumph over the temptation of power. Faramir becomes an ally to Frodo and Sam, offering his support and wisdom in their difficult task, an act of bravery that shows that not everyone has been corrupted by evil. The path to Mordor remains uncertain, but with Faramir's help and Sam's unwavering loyalty, Frodo feels one step closer to fulfilling his destiny, as darkness lurks at every step.

Part IV:
The Final Battle and the Fate of the Ring

As the story builds to its climax, Middle-earth is plunged into an epic war that will define its destiny. The armies of light prepare for the final battle against the dark forces of Sauron , while Frodo and Sam continue their perilous journey to Mount Doom, the only place where the One Ring can be destroyed. Tension and uncertainty mount, as the fate of Middle-earth hangs in the balance. Hope and despair intertwine as the characters prepare to give their all in this momentous struggle.

The final battle is fought at Minas Tirith , the capital of Gondor , where the armies of Men, led by Gandalf and Aragorn , face off against Sauron 's hordes of Orcs and other evil creatures . The battle is fierce and desperate, with significant losses on both sides. Aragorn , with his leadership and courage, becomes a symbol of hope for Men, as he fights to protect his people from the darkness. The arrival of reinforcements from Rohan, led by Éomer , and the support of the Elves, bring new forces to the battle, but the Orcs' numerical superiority remains a great threat. The fate of Middle-earth is decided in this epic battle, in which the courage and resolve of the heroes are put to the test.

Meanwhile, further afield, Frodo and Sam, guided by Gollum , approach Mount Doom, where they must finally fulfill their quest. The journey is dangerous and grueling, and the corrupting power of the ring takes an increasing toll on Frodo, who struggles to resist the temptation to use the ring for himself. The presence of Gollum , with his two conflicting personalities, adds constant tension, as the hobbits must remain vigilant about their actions and plans. The difficulty of the journey becomes more apparent with each step, but Frodo and Sam's friendship and determination keep them going.

Gollum 's betrayal is revealed when he attempts to steal the ring from Frodo, but ends up falling into the abyss in his attempt. Meanwhile, Frodo manages to reach the edge of the volcano, the place where the One Ring was forged, but at the last moment, the power of the ring corrupts him and he refuses to destroy it. However, fate intervenes in an unexpected way: Gollum reappears and in the fight for the ring, bites Frodo's finger, taking the ring with him, to fall into the lava of Mount Doom, destroying it forever. The destruction of the ring marks the end of Sauron 's reign and his evil, freeing Middle-earth from his shadow. The destruction of the ring becomes an act that seals the fate of Middle-earth, ending the reign of evil and darkness.

With the defeat of Sauron , the forces of darkness fade and Middle-earth is freed from their threat. Aragorn is crowned King of Gondor , uniting Men and leading them into a new era of peace and prosperity. The Elves, seeing the restoration of the kingdom, decide to leave Middle-earth to return to the lands of the gods, ushering in the age of Men. The end of the war marks a new beginning for the peoples of Middle-earth, who begin a path towards peace and reconstruction. Peace and prosperity return to Middle-earth following the defeat of Sauron , a symbol of the victory of light over darkness.

Frodo, although he managed to accomplish his mission, is scarred by the physical and emotional wounds caused by the ring. Together with his friend Bilbo and some elves, he embarks for the Undying

Lands, a place of peace and rest, where he hopes to heal the wounds of his heart. Sam, Merry and Pippin, meanwhile, return to the Shire, where they are welcomed as heroes and enjoy a peaceful and happy life. Frodo's story ends with his departure for the lands of the gods, an act that marks the end of an era in Middle-earth.

Friendship, courage and hope stand out as the values that allow the characters to overcome the challenges they face and achieve final victory. The sacrifice of many, the loyalty of a few and the courage of all marked the history and destiny of Middle-earth, where light triumphed over darkness, and a new path was opened for the future. The story of The Lord of the Rings ends with the triumph of light over darkness, leaving a message of hope and the victory of good over evil in the hearts of all.

The Battle of Helm's Deep

The threat of darkness looms over Middle-earth, and the battle for survival rages at Helm's Deep. The people of Rohan seek refuge in this fortified place, seeking protection from the relentless advance of Saruman 's forces. Aragorn 's arrival at Helm's Deep marks a turning point in the story, as his presence inspires hope and courage amidst chaos and despair. Aragorn , aware of the danger they face, assumes leadership of the defense, rallying the warriors and preparing the fortifications to withstand the enemy onslaught. Aragorn 's arrival becomes a symbol of resistance, as his presence inspires confidence in the hearts of those preparing for battle.

The Orcish attack on Helm's Deep is fierce and merciless. Saruman 's hordes , led by his fearsome Uruk-hai , charge against the walls with brutal force, seeking to crush the defenders' resistance. The battle is bloody and merciless, with significant casualties on both sides. The warriors of Rohan, alongside Aragorn , fight with bravery and courage, but the Orcs' numerical superiority puts them in a desperate situation. The defense of Helm's Deep becomes a fight for survival, where every moment counts and every life matters. Aragorn faces the Orcs with courage, demonstrating his skill as a warrior and his commitment to the defense of the realm.

In the midst of the battle, a ray of hope emerges with the unexpected arrival of the elves, who come to the aid of their allies. The presence of these ancient warriors, with their skill and wisdom, brings new strength to the defense of Helm's Deep. The elves, led by Legolas , demonstrate their skill with the bow and their bravery in combat, pushing back the enemy forces at several strategic points. The participation of the elves becomes an example of the union of the free races of Middle-earth against darkness, a moment that highlights the importance of collaboration in times of crisis. The aid of the elves marks a turning point in the battle, as their skills and bravery provide respite to the defenders.

As the night draws on, the situation at Helm's Deep becomes increasingly critical, with the defenders on the brink of defeat. However, just as all hope seems lost, a saving figure appears on the horizon. The arrival of Gandalf at dawn, accompanied by reinforcements from Rohan led by Éomer , turns the tide of the battle. Gandalf, with his magic and wisdom, leads the cavalry charge, unleashing a whirlwind of destruction upon Saruman 's forces . Gandalf's arrival becomes a symbol of hope, as his presence marks the start of the counter-offensive. The appearance of Gandalf and the reinforcements from Rohan marks a turning point in the battle, providing a new impetus to the defenders' resistance.

The arrival of Gandalf's reinforcements sparks a decisive counteroffensive, allowing the defenders of Helm's Deep to drive the orcs back and force them to flee in disarray. The battle ends in victory for the free people, who prove that unity and courage are stronger than darkness. The Battle of Helm's Deep becomes a symbol of the free people's resistance to tyranny, a victory that inspires hope in the fight against darkness. Victory at Helm's Deep marks a pivotal moment in the war, proving that hope can triumph over despair.

Yet despite the victory, the war is not yet over, and dangers continue to lurk in Middle-earth. Aragorn , Gandalf, and the other heroes must prepare for the next challenge, knowing that the fate of the world remains at stake. The Battle of Helm's Deep marks a turning point in the war against Saruman , a moment of victory that renews hope in the fight against the darkness. The Battle of Helm's Deep ends in triumph for the defenders, but the war against the darkness is far from over.

The Attack of the Ents and the Fall of Isengard

In Middle-earth, as war rages, a momentous event unfolds that changes the course of history: the Ent attack on Isengard . This chapter chronicles Merry and Pippin 's encounter with Treebeard , the Ent leader , and the subsequent destruction of Saruman 's fortress , marking a turning point in the fight against the darkness. After escaping the orcs who had captured them, Merry and Pippin venture into Fangorn Forest , where they encounter Treebeard , an ancient tree-like being who becomes an unlikely ally.

Treebeard , initially wary of the hobbits, becomes curious about their presence and decides to listen to them. Merry and Pippin explain to him the state of the war and Saruman 's role in spreading evil, which arouses the fury of Treebeard and his people. The Ents , ancient and peaceful beings, have long watched as the forests are destroyed by the ambitions of Men and Orcs, but their slowness to act has prevented them from taking drastic measures until now. The arrival of Merry and Pippin becomes the catalyst that ignites the Ents ' anger and leads them to take up arms. The history of deforestation near Isengard infuriates Treebeard and he decides to join the war against Saruman .

Determined to avenge the destruction of their forests, Treebeard calls all the Ents to a meeting where they debate whether to join the war. The decision is not easy, as the Ents are slow to make decisions, but their outrage at Saruman 's betrayal overcomes their reluctance. After much discussion, the Ents decide that it is time to act and that their peaceful way of life must change in the face of the threat looming over Middle-earth. The meeting of the Ents becomes a key moment in history, as it marks the beginning of their intervention in the war against evil. The Ents are powerful and ancient beings, and their entry into the conflict represents a threat to Saruman's plans.

Thus, the Ents move towards Isengard, Saruman's fortress, led by Treebeard, leaving behind their traditional slowness and adopting a combative attitude. The march of the Ents towards Isengard is a demonstration of their power, since their presence imposes respect and fear. With their enormous strength and unleashed fury, they destroy everything in their path, knocking down walls and destroying war machines. Saruman's fortress, which had previously seemed impregnable, falls before the attack of the enraged Ents. The destruction of Isengard is an example of the power of nature when it rises up against destruction.

The destruction of Isengard by the Ents is a key event in the war against Saruman, as it marks the end of their power and influence in Middle-earth. The fortress, which was a symbol of their evil and ambition, is reduced to rubble by the Ents' force. With the fall of Isengard, Saruman is stripped of his weapons and resources, weakening his position and driving him even further from his goals. The fall of Isengard also represents a victory for the forces of light, who see one of the main bastions of darkness defeated.

Merry and Pippin, who witness the fury of the Ents, become witnesses of a historic moment that changes the course of the war. Their encounter with Treebeard and their participation in the subsequent events mark a turning point in their lives, transforming them into heroes who contribute to the salvation of Middle-earth. After the Ents destroy the dam and flood everything, they take a break, while Merry and Pippin play happily in the water, which makes them grow.

The fall of Isengard is not only a military victory, but also a symbol of nature's justice and vengeance against the evil of man. The Ents , who had always maintained a peaceful attitude, demonstrate that even the calmest of beings can rise up in defense of what they love. Their action against Isengard is an example of the power that lies in nature and how nature can respond to man's aggression. The destruction of Isengard by the Ents is a decisive moment in the war against Saruman , which also symbolizes nature's justice against the evil and greed of men.

The Siege of Minas Tirith

In Middle-earth, the shadow of war looms over Minas Tirith , the citadel of Gondor , ushering in a siege that will test the endurance of men and the sanity of their leaders. This chapter focuses on the despair gripping the city, the madness of Steward Denethor, and the arrival of reinforcements from Rohan, a ray of hope in the darkness. Steward Denethor, a man of great power and wisdom but consumed by despair and pride, is revealed to be a ruler incapable of dealing with the impending invasion of the forces of Mordor. His madness is manifested in his cruel treatment of his son, Faramir, and his refusal to call upon other kingdoms for aid, blinded by arrogance and the belief that Gondor can defeat the looming threat alone.

The attack on Minas Tirith is unleashed with unprecedented ferocity, with hordes of orcs and evil creatures storming the walls of the citadel. Desperation spreads among the defenders, who, faced with the numerical superiority of the enemy and the lack of leadership of the seneschal, see defeat as inevitable. The city becomes chaotic, with fires and destruction everywhere, while the inhabitants fight for their lives. The situation worsens with the advance of the Witch-king of Angmar, the leader of the Nazgûl , who commands the dark forces with his power and generates terror in the hearts of men.

In the midst of the battle, Faramir, the seneschal's son, demonstrates his bravery and nobility by leading a group of soldiers in a desperate attempt to defend the city. However, his forces are outnumbered and he himself is severely wounded. Upon returning to the city, he finds his father insane, who shows no concern for his well-being. Denethor's unfair and merciless treatment of Faramir, rather than showing gratitude for his sacrifice, reveals the depth of his mental imbalance. This attitude of the seneschal also shows that he preferred his son Boromir .

Denethor's madness reaches its climax when, faced with imminent defeat, he decides to burn himself and his wounded son on a funeral pyre. This decision, motivated by fear and despair, is an act of madness and hopelessness that demonstrates his inability to lead Gondor in its darkest hour. Gandalf, seeing what is happening, tries to stop him, but is too late to save the steward. Denethor is consumed by the flames, but Faramir, thanks to the intervention of Pippin , is rescued from the flames in time.

In the midst of the desolation, when all seems lost, reinforcements from Rohan arrive, riding across the plains to join the fight against the darkness. Their arrival marks a turning point in the battle, instilling hope in the hearts of the defenders and turning the tide of the fight. The riders of Rohan, led by King Théoden, charge into battle with unstoppable ferocity, proving their loyalty and bravery. Éowyn , the king's niece, also joins the battle alongside Merry, proving her courage. King Théoden is killed in the battle and Éowyn , alongside Merry, fights against the Witch-king of Angmar, and it is the latter who, with the help of the hobbit, defeats him.

The arrival of reinforcements from Rohan reinvigorates the forces of Gondor and gives them new impetus to fight against the darkness, although the armies of Mordor are still more numerous. The battle continues with renewed intensity, with both sides fighting with all their might. Despite the losses suffered, the alliance between men and elves remains strong, and their resistance proves that hope is not yet lost. Aragorn also arrives with reinforcements and leads the once-human wraiths who are forced to fight for him. With this help, men and elves win a victory against the armies of Mordor.

The Siege of Minas Tirith is a pivotal moment in the war for Middle-earth, where hope and despair, madness and bravery collide in an epic battle. Despite the losses and suffering, the resilience of Gondor's defenders and the arrival of reinforcements from Rohan mark a turning point in the conflict, proving that even in the darkest hour, the light of hope can re-emerge.

The Road to Mountain Doom

The narrative follows hobbits Frodo and Sam on their arduous journey into the heart of Mordor, while also focusing on the events that lead to Aragorn claiming his heritage and leading an army into the final battle. The paths of these characters intertwine, though geographically separated, in a struggle against the power of evil and despair.

Exhausted and hungry, Frodo and Sam continue their journey through the barren and dangerous wilderness surrounding Mordor. Their path is made even more difficult by the presence of Gollum , who, although initially guiding them, also plans to betray them in order to keep the Ring for himself. Mistrust between Sam and Gollum grows as the latter attempts to manipulate Frodo, sowing doubts about his friend's loyalty. Despite these difficulties, Frodo's determination to fulfill his mission remains firm, although the Ring begins to exert an increasing influence over him.

The hobbits' journey takes them into a dark tunnel where they encounter the giant spider Shelob , a monstrous creature that attacks them. In this encounter, Frodo is stung by Shelob and left paralyzed. It is then that Sam, driven by his loyalty and love for Frodo, engages the spider in a fierce battle, using Galadriel 's sword and light to defend his friend. Sam manages to rescue Frodo from Shelob 's clutches , but the two are separated when the orcs capture Frodo and carry off his body.

Sam, believing Frodo dead, decides to take the Ring with the intention of completing the quest on his own. However, upon hearing Orcs speak of Frodo being alive, Sam realises there is still hope and decides to go after him. Bravely, Sam infiltrates the Orc stronghold, rescues Frodo, and together they continue their journey to Mount Doom, although the Ring exerts an ever-stronger hold on Frodo.

Meanwhile, elsewhere in Middle-earth, Aragorn is facing his own destiny. Following the battle at Helm's Deep, Aragorn sets out on a journey to reclaim his heritage as King of Gondor . To do so, he must seek out an army of mountain-dwelling wraiths who in the past betrayed Isildur . Accompanied by Legolas and Gimli, Aragorn sets out into the Path of the Dead to convince these wraiths to fight by his side. Aragorn manages to convince the wraiths to aid him in battle, displaying the sword that once belonged to Isildur , proving his royal lineage and the legitimacy of his claim.

At a crucial moment, Aragorn , along with the army of wraiths, arrives on shore and boards a fleet of corsair ships. This fleet, which was headed to aid the forces of Mordor, becomes a reinforcement army for Gondor . With this fleet, Aragorn heads to the Black Gate of Mordor, where the final battle takes place. There, the forces of Gondor , led by Gandalf, Aragorn , and other heroes, engage Sauron 's army in desperate combat, giving Frodo and Sam time to reach Mountain Doom.

At the Black Gate, the battle rages, with both sides fighting with all their might. Gandalf calls upon the eagles to aid in the fight, while humans and wraiths engage the orcs. In the midst of the battle, Aragorn is tempted by Sauron , but remains steadfast in his determination to defeat evil. The battle becomes a necessary distraction to allow Frodo and Sam a chance to complete their quest at Mount Doom. The events of this chapter demonstrate that bravery and loyalty are powerful forces, even in the face of darkness and despair.

The Destruction of the Ring

The narrative reaches its climax with the destruction of the One Ring, the defeat of Sauron , and the rescue of Frodo and Sam, marking the end of the epic struggle for Middle-earth. Events rush toward a conclusion, where hope and despair collide in a final battle for the fate of the world.

Frodo and Sam, after overcoming countless dangers, finally reach Mount Doom, the only place where the Ring can be destroyed. As they get closer to their goal, the power of the Ring grows stronger, corrupting Frodo's mind. Upon reaching the edge of the Crack of Doom, Frodo refuses to destroy the Ring, succumbing to its influence and claiming it as his own. This desperate act reveals the magnitude of temptation and the difficulty of resisting the Ring's power. Frodo's will, weakened by the long journey and the constant struggle against darkness, finally gives in to the power of evil.

In a moment of chaos and despair, Gollum appears , obsessed with retrieving the Ring. In a frantic struggle with Frodo, Gollum bites off Frodo's finger, retrieving the Ring. However, in his euphoria, Gollum loses his balance and falls into the lava of Mount Doom, dying in the process. With Gollum 's fall , the Ring is destroyed, causing a shockwave felt throughout Middle-earth. Sauron 's power fades, his armies are thrown into disarray and defeated. Thus, Gollum 's selfish act becomes the catalyst for the Ring's destruction, an ironic twist of fate.

The destruction of the Ring marks the defeat of Sauron . His tower at Barad-dûr collapses, and his evil power is eradicated from Middle-earth. His armies, bereft of their leader, are scattered and defeated by the forces of good. Gandalf and his allies celebrate their victory, knowing that they have triumphed over the darkness. Sauron's armies, including the orcs, uruk-hai, and other evil creatures, are soundly defeated. Sauron's fall not only marks the end of his reign of terror, but also ushers in a new era of peace and hope.

Meanwhile, Frodo and Sam are stranded on a rock in the middle of the erupting volcano, giving up. Despair grips them at the thought of their impending death. However, Gandalf, with the help of the eagles, rescues them from Mount Doom, taking them to safety. Frodo and Sam are hailed as heroes, though Frodo bears the burden of not having destroyed the Ring of his own free will. His journey and sacrifice are acknowledged by all, who understand the magnitude of his bravery. Despite the after-effects of his traumatic experience, Frodo finds comfort in knowing that he has accomplished his mission.

The rescue of Frodo and Sam marks the end of their dangerous quest. They are taken to Minas Tirith, where they receive a grand welcome, marking the beginning of the rebuilding of Middle-earth. With the destruction of the Ring and the defeat of Sauron, Middle-earth is freed from his shadow, and a new era of peace and hope begins. The sacrifice of the hobbits and their companions is fundamental to the victory over evil, highlighting the importance of friendship, loyalty and bravery.

The chapter closes with the dawn of a new era in Middle-earth, where peace and prosperity begin to replace the fear and darkness that had long held sway. Heroes are celebrated and honored, but the true triumph lies in the sacrifice and bravery of those who fought against the darkness, marking the end of a long and dangerous journey.

Part V:
The Return and the End

The story focuses on the return of the heroes and the establishment of a new order in Middle-earth, marking the end of their epic journey. The main characters return to their homes, and victories are celebrated, but the emotional and physical wounds of war are also faced. Peace is restored, and an era of reconstruction and hope is ushered in.

Following the destruction of the Ring and the defeat of Sauron , the heroes return to Rivendell , where victory is celebrated. Here, Frodo is reunited with Bilbo , who gives him the book he had begun to write, which Frodo continued during his journey to Mordor. This book becomes a record of their adventures and sacrifices. The fellowship gathers together to share stories and to honour those who fought in the war against Sauron . Aragorn prepares to ascend the throne of Gondor as the rightful king.

Aragorn is crowned King of Gondor , fulfilling his destiny as Isildur 's heir . His reign marks the beginning of a new era of justice and prosperity in Middle-earth. Aragorn shows humility by acknowledging the hobbits for their bravery and sacrifice, declaring that they should never bow down to anyone. This declaration demonstrates the respect and gratitude he feels for them. His coronation unites the kingdoms of men and ushers in an era of peace and cooperation.

The hobbits return to their homeland of the Shire, where they are welcomed as heroes, though they learn little of what happened. Sam marries his beloved and raises a family, finding happiness in the simple life of the Shire. Despite all they have been through, the hobbits return to their everyday lives, though they are profoundly changed by their experiences. Their acts of bravery and loyalty inspire all the inhabitants of Middle-earth.

Meanwhile, Frodo cannot find the peace he was looking for, as the wounds from the Ring continue to affect him. The weight of the burden he carried torments him, and he feels the need to find a place where he can rest. Therefore, like Bilbo , Frodo decides to leave for Valinor , the Undying Lands, a place where elves go at the end of their days and where, thanks to Arwen's intervention, hobbits can also go.

At the port, Frodo says goodbye to his friends Sam, Merry and Pippin , knowing that they will not see each other again. With emotional words, Frodo hands the book to Sam, who must continue the story of his adventures. The hobbits say goodbye with the sadness of parting, but with the certainty that they have fulfilled their mission with honor and courage. Frodo's departure symbolizes the end of an era and the beginning of another, where the memory of his sacrifice will endure forever. Frodo, together with Bilbo , Gandalf and the last elves, embark for Valinor .

Finally, Sam returns home and begins a new stage in his life. The text ends with the idea that Sam stays at home "to live happily ever after", reflecting the hope and peace that was restored to Middle-earth after Sauron 's defeat .

The Return Home

The story focuses on the heroes' return to their homes and the establishment of a new order in Middle-earth, marking the end of their epic adventure. The main characters return to their lives, victories are celebrated, and the emotional and physical scars left by the war are dealt with. Peace is restored, giving way to an era of reconstruction and hope.

Following the destruction of the One Ring and the defeat of Sauron , the heroes return to Rivendell , where a celebration of their victory is held. Here Frodo is reunited with Bilbo , who gives him the book he had begun to write and which Frodo continued during his journey to Mordor. This book becomes a testament to their adventures and sacrifices. The fellowship comes together to share stories and honour those who fought in the war against Sauron . Aragorn prepares to ascend the throne of Gondor as the rightful king.

Aragorn is crowned King of Gondor , fulfilling his destiny as Isildur 's heir . His reign ushers in a new era of justice and prosperity in Middle-earth. Aragorn shows humility by commendation to the hobbits for their bravery and sacrifice, declaring that they should never bow down to anyone. This declaration demonstrates the respect and gratitude he feels for them. His coronation unites the kingdoms of men and ushers in an era of peace and cooperation.

The hobbits return to their home in the Shire, where they are welcomed as heroes, though no one in these parts knows anything about them. Sam marries his beloved and raises a family, finding happiness in the simple life of the Shire. Despite all they have been through, the hobbits return to their everyday lives, though they have been profoundly changed by the experiences they have faced. Their acts of bravery and loyalty inspire all the inhabitants of Middle-earth.

Meanwhile, Frodo cannot find the peace he was looking for, as the wounds from the Ring continue to affect him. The weight of the burden he carried torments him, and he feels the need to find a place where he can rest. Therefore, like Bilbo , Frodo decides to leave for Valinor , the Undying Lands, a place where the elves go at the end of their days and where, thanks to Arwen's intervention, the hobbits can also go.

At the port, Frodo says goodbye to his friends Sam, Merry and Pippin , knowing that they will not see each other again. With emotional words, Frodo hands the book to Sam, who must continue the story of his adventures. The hobbits say goodbye with the sadness of parting, but with the certainty that they have fulfilled their mission with honor and courage. Frodo's departure symbolizes the end of an era and the beginning of another, where the memory of his sacrifice will endure forever. Frodo, together with Bilbo , Gandalf and the last elves, embark for Valinor .

Finally, Sam returns home and begins a new chapter in his life. The text ends with the idea that Sam stays at home "to live happily ever after," reflecting the hope and peace that was restored to Middle-earth after Sauron 's defeat . His story, like that of the other hobbits, is proof that bravery and friendship can overcome even the greatest darkness.

This chapter shows how the heroes return to their homes after a long and dangerous adventure. Aragorn 's coronation brings a new era of peace to Middle-earth, and the hobbits return to the Shire where they are honoured for their deeds. Frodo and Bilbo 's departure for Valinor marks an end, but also a new beginning for Middle-earth. Sam, despite his sadness at his friend's departure, returns home and builds a happy and peaceful life.

Epilogue

The story explores the characters' individual fates after the Great War, offering reflections on the saga's central themes. It reveals how their lived experiences shape their future lives and considers the enduring lessons the story offers its readers. The epilogue serves as a closure to the characters' adventures, but also invites reflection on good and evil, the power of friendship, and courage in the face of adversity.

Following the destruction of the One Ring and the defeat of Sauron , Middle-earth enters a new era of peace and rebuilding. The destinies of the main characters become intertwined with this new landscape, each following their own path influenced by the trials they faced. Aragorn , now crowned King Elessar , begins his reign with wisdom and justice, guiding Gondor into an era of prosperity and collaboration. His leadership unifies the peoples of Middle-earth, laying the foundation for peaceful coexistence between Men, Elves, and Dwarves. Aragorn also joins Arwen, who gives up her immortality to be at his side, sealing their love with a commitment that defies the barriers between the races.

As for the hobbits, their return to the Shire marks a return to the simplicity of rural life. Sam marries his beloved and raises a family, finding joy in everyday chores and the love of his children. His life reflects the importance of humility and contentment in the small things. Merry and Pippin , on the other hand, become respected figures in the Shire, renowned for their participation in the war and their adventures. Despite their fame, they never forget their roots and remain the cheerful and curious hobbits they have always been.

Frodo, however, finds inner peace harder to come by. The physical and emotional wounds he sustained during his journey to Mordor linger, leaving him with a deep sense of restlessness and a longing for healing. The weight of the Ring and his proximity to darkness have marked him indelibly. He makes the decision to set out for Valinor , seeking a place of rest and healing with Bilbo , Gandalf, and the last of the Elves. Arwen gives up her place to Frodo so that he may go to the undying lands to heal. Her departure symbolizes a melancholic closure, but also represents the promise of a new stage, free from pain and sorrow. Her sacrifice is a testament to the resilience of the spirit and the search for inner peace.

The epilogue also takes time to reflect on the deeper themes explored in the series. The struggle between good and evil, the corrupting nature of power, and the importance of friendship and courage are recurring elements that resonate throughout the story. The idea that even the smallest and seemingly insignificant beings, such as hobbits, can play a crucial role in the fate of the world is highlighted. Loyalty, sacrifice, and the ability to persevere in the face of adversity are virtues that are exalted and offer a guide for life.

The One Ring, a symbol of power and corruption, becomes a metaphor for the dangers of uncontrolled desire and temptation. The story shows that true power lies in the ability to choose the good, even when it is difficult and involves sacrifice. The hobbits' humility and willingness to put the welfare of others before their own interests makes them true heroes.

Furthermore, the importance of hope is emphasized, even in the darkest of times. The saga shows that light can prevail over darkness, but this requires the effort and determination of all those who choose to fight for good. The fight against evil is not an individual battle, but a collective effort that requires the cooperation and solidarity of different peoples and races.

The epilogue also offers a reflection on the passage of time and change. The departure of the elves and the rise of men as the principal inhabitants of Middle-earth mark the end of one era and the beginning of another. The history of Middle-earth is not static, but a constant process of transformation and adaptation. The saga teaches us that, although change can be painful, it is also necessary for growth and progress.

In the ending, Sam inherits the book that Bilbo started and Frodo continued, symbolizing the continuity of the story and the legacy of their adventures. Sam returns to the Shire where he lives happily ever after with his family, a testament that happiness and peace are found in the simple things. The fates of all the characters are intertwined in this narrative, reminding us that every action, no matter how small, can have a lasting impact on the world.

The epilogue offers an in-depth look at the characters' individual fates following the fall of Sauron . From Aragorn 's reign to Frodo's departure for Valinor , the saga explores the themes of friendship, sacrifice, the fight against evil, and hope. The hobbits' journey, Aragorn 's coronation , and Frodo's decision to depart are all components of a cohesive narrative that underscores the importance of bravery, humility, and perseverance. As it concludes, the story leaves a reflection on the nature of power and the responsibility it carries, inviting readers to consider the lessons of Middle-earth in their own lives. The characters' fates are intertwined, highlighting that every action counts in the pursuit of good.

Final Note

Aragorn's coronation as King of Gondor, ushering in a new era of peace and justice in Middle-earth. His reign unifies the peoples, establishing a collaboration between Men, Elves, and Dwarves, who have fought together against the darkness of Sauron. Aragorn, also known as Strider, is the heir of Isildur, the king who defeated Sauron, and is revealed to be a strong and wise leader, whose leadership is critical to the prosperity of Gondor. His coronation represents not only the fulfillment of a prophecy, but also hope for a better future for Middle-earth.

The hobbits, who played a crucial role in the defeat of Sauron, return to the Shire, where they are welcomed as heroes, although daily life there does not change much. Sam, Frodo's most faithful companion, marries his beloved and raises a family, finding happiness in the simplicity of rural life. Merry and Pippin also return to the Shire, where they are viewed with respect due to their participation in the war. Despite their experiences, they never forget their roots, remaining the cheerful and curious hobbits they have always been.

Frodo, however, does not find the peace he sought, for the wounds of the Ring persist. The weight of the burden he carried torments him, and he feels the need to find a place where he can rest. Therefore, like Bilbo, Frodo decides to leave for Valinor, the Undying Lands, a place where elves go at the end of their days, and where, thanks to Arwen's intervention, hobbits can also go. At the port, Frodo says goodbye to his friends with emotional words, giving the book to Sam so that he can continue the story. His departure symbolizes a melancholic end but represents the promise of a new stage, free of pain and sadness.

Sam returns home and begins a new chapter in his life, with the idea of "living happily ever after", which reflects the hope and peace that was restored to Middle-earth after the defeat of Sauron . Sam inherits Bilbo and Frodo 's book , which symbolizes the continuation of the story and the legacy of their adventures. The story of each character, although different, is intertwined in a cohesive narrative that underlines the importance of bravery, humility and perseverance. The saga, in its entirety, is a reflection on power, sacrifice, friendship and the struggle between good and evil.

Furthermore, the importance of hope is highlighted, even in the darkest of times. The saga shows that light can prevail over darkness, but this requires the effort and determination of all those who choose to fight for good. The fight against evil is not an individual battle, but a collective effort that requires the cooperation and solidarity of different peoples and races. The text explores the destinies of the characters after the great war, revealing how the experiences lived shape their future lives and offering a reflection on the importance of friendship and courage in the face of adversity. The story also explores the passage of time and change, revealing that the history of Middle-earth is a constant process of transformation and adaptation.

The Lord of the Rings saga culminates in a sense of hope and peace, where the characters' destinies have been fulfilled. From Aragorn 's reign to Frodo's departure for Valinor , the narrative underlines the importance of bravery, humility and perseverance. The story of the hobbits, as well as that of the other characters, is a testament to the fact that even the smallest and most insignificant can play a crucial role in the fate of the world.

Curiosities

"J.R.R. Tolkien's work transcended his own medium, inspiring musicians, filmmakers, illustrators and game designers, influencing creations such as 'Dungeons and Dragons' and 'Game of Thrones'."

-

"The 'Lord of the Rings' trilogy of fantasy novels was published between 1954 and 1955 as a sequel to 1937's 'The Hobbit'."

-

"Unlike 'The Hobbit,' 'The Lord of the Rings' was a work for hire by the publisher, as Tolkien had no interest in continuing his earlier novel."

-

"Prior to the Peter Jackson films, there were two animated films: one by Ralph Bakshi in 1978, which covered part of 'The Fellowship of the Ring,' and another by Jules Bass and Arthur Rankin Jr. in 1980, 'The Return of the King,' a musical for the whole family."

-

"Peter Jackson's trilogy was released between 2001 and 2003, being a watershed in film history."

"The first film in Peter Jackson's trilogy grossed more than $871 billion at the worldwide box office and won four Oscars."

-

"The cast of Peter Jackson's films included Elijah Wood as Frodo, Ian Holm as Bilbo, Sean Astin as Sam, Viggo Mortensen as Aragorn, Ian McKellen as Gandalf, Liv Tyler as Arwen, Orlando Bloom as Legolas and Christopher Lee as Saruman."

-

"Christopher Lee was the only cast member who knew J.R.R. Tolkien and would read the trilogy annually until his death in 2015."

-

"March 25 is known worldwide as 'Read Tolkien Day,' promoted by The Tolkien Society."

-

"Tolkien despised Walt Disney and did not want him to adapt his works to film."

-

"'The Lord of the Rings' is the film saga with the most Oscar nominations, racking up 30 nominations and winning 17."

"The total running time of 'The Lord of the Rings' trilogy is 8 hours and 27 minutes, and 11 hours and 21 minutes in its extended versions."

-

"Led Zeppelin was the first band to deliberately include references to 'The Lord of the Rings' in their lyrics."

-

"Originally, 'The Lord of the Rings' was planned as a single volume, but was split into three due to rising paper prices."

-

"The subtitles for each volume were not Tolkien's idea, and the only one he liked was 'The Fellowship of the Ring'."

-

"C.S. Lewis, a friend of Tolkien's, was an early reader of the work and motivated him to continue developing it."

-

"In the late 1960s, hippies popularized graffiti and pins with slogans related to the work, even though Tolkien despised them."

"If you read in reverse order the number of rings the races received, you get 1973, the year Tolkien died."

-

"The first attempt to adapt the work to video games was a Parker Brothers title for the Atari 2600, which was cancelled and found 20 years later."

-

"Stanley Kubrick wanted to direct a 'Lord of the Rings' film in 1969, but Tolkien rejected the idea."

-

"The Beatles had planned to participate in Kubrick's adaptation, with Lennon as Gollum, McCartney as Frodo, Harrison as Gandalf and Starr as Sam."

-

"Pope Francis is a fan of Tolkien's work."

-

"Stephen King was inspired by 'The Lord of the Rings' for his 'The Dark Tower' saga."

-

"Ian Holm, who played Bilbo in Peter Jackson's films, voiced Frodo in a 1981 BBC radio dramatization."

-

"A producer of Peter Jackson's films wanted a hobbit to die."

-

"Sean Connery turned down the role of Gandalf, and Nicolas Cage turned down the role of Aragorn."

-

"The 'Lord of the Rings' trilogy cost less than 'The Hobbit' trilogy."

-

"All the mountains on Titan, Saturn's largest moon, are named after 'Lord of the Rings' mountains."

-

"Tolkien's son Christopher disliked Peter Jackson's film version to the point of refusing to meet him."

-

"Tolkien served in the British navy during World War I and his experiences influenced the rawest scenes in the play."

Legal Notice and Copyright

Copyright © 2025 Editorial Nova. All rights reserved.

This book and its contents, including text, images, design, graphics and any other material, are protected by applicable intellectual property and copyright laws.

The reproduction, distribution, modification, transmission, exhibition or any other total or partial use of this material is strictly prohibited without the express written authorization of Editorial Nova.

Exceptions permitted by law, such as personal and non-commercial use, quotation for educational or review purposes, must always include the corresponding acknowledgment to the publisher and author.

Disclaimer

The information contained in this publication is for informational and/or educational purposes. Although every effort has been made to ensure that it is accurate and up-to-date, neither the author nor Editorial Nova assumes responsibility for misinterpretations, decisions or actions taken based on the contents of the book.

If this material contains references to actual brands, products, persons or events, these are included for illustrative purposes only and do not imply any affiliation, endorsement or legal relationship with Editorial Nova.

⊙ nova

www.ingramcontent.com/pod-product-compliance
Lightning Source LLC
LaVergne TN
LVHW012034060526
838201LV00061B/4595